Introduction

This book is a collection of patterns that take advantage of self-striping sock yarns to transform simple knitting into show-stopping accessories.

Remember the first time you saw self-striping sock yarn? Whether it was a sample at your yarn store or in a friend's knitting bag, your initial response was probably "You're kidding!" quickly followed by "How do they do that?"

Over the past five years many knitters have made socks for the first time, inspired by the varied stripe patterns and wonderful colorways available. Making a complicated-looking project using only basic knitting—what's not to like? In this book, we explore what comes after socks.

This is not a "how to knit" book. The patterns use common techniques which can be found in any good knitting reference. My favorite is Knitter's Companion, from Interweave Press.

All of these projects are well within the reach of an adventurous beginner. The yarn provides the complexity, allowing the knitting to be kept simple. Most of the projects are small, so it won't take forever to finish. Don't be scared off by the small gauge. Grab your needles and dive in!

Not just Socks

Sandi Rosner

Editorial Director   David Codling

Editor and Graphic Design   Gregory Courtney

Photography   Kathryn Martin

Makeup and Hair Styling   Kira Lee

Models   Myra Slattery, Michelle Rich, Joel Broderick,
Sara Jane Farrell and "Sidney"

Color Reproduction and Printing   Regent Publishing Services

Published and Distributed By   Unicorn Books and Crafts, Inc.

Printed in China

ISBN   1-893063-10-0

2 3 4 5 6 7 8 9 10

Thoughts on Working with Self-striping Sock Yarns

〰 You don't have to use the colors in your yarn in the order they appear. Feel free to manipulate the color placement to please yourself. If you want green thumbs on your mittens, just wind off some yarn until you get to the green section. If you want your ribbed edges in a solid color, just wind off the spotted part.

〰 Pay attention to the sequence of colors in your yarn. If you want the pieces of a pair to match, you will want to make sure the colors appear in the same order. When you start a new ball of yarn, make sure the colors run in the same direction. Rarely, but sometimes, the sequence will reverse from skein to skein, even within the same dye lot. You may need to work one skein from the outside and the next from the inside strand in order to keep the sequence consistent.

〰 Some people love the look of an unmatched pair. For others, it just makes them crazy. You know who you are. If you want your pair to match, start the first piece at the junction between two colors. Wind off yarn to get to the same place in the color sequence when you start the second piece. If an unmatched look is more your style, just start wherever you are and let the colors fall as they may. Both approaches are reflected in the projects in this book.

〰 Remember that tiny changes in tension will affect how the colors in your yarn line up, particularly in the spotted sections. The spots may stack in one stripe, and form chevrons in another. Don't make yourself nuts trying to control this. Embrace serendipity! Allow your project to delight you with its idiosyncrasies.

〰 Don't get your heart set on a particular color or style of self-striping sock yarn. These yarns are fashion items and change every season. For this reason a number of projects are shown in more than one colorway. If the colorway used isn't available, try a different one! Have fun exploring the possibilities.

Scarves

Scarves

Scarves

Scarves

Scarves

Scarves

Scarves

DIFFICULTY EASY

YARN LANA GROSSA MEILENWEIT FANTASY (200 GRAMS)

NEEDLES SHORT US 3 (3.25 MM) *OR THE SIZE YOU NEED TO GET GAUGE*

MEASUREMENTS 8" × 85"

Gauge 24 sts and 32 rows = 4" in garter stitch

Although this scarf has a rich, autumnal feeling, the mood will change dramatically depending on the colorway you choose. Each diamond-shaped module is knit separately, using stitches picked up from neighboring diamonds.

Note
Follow the diagram on page 12 and the instructions for squares and triangles on page 13 to make the scarf in two identical halves as follows:

Modular Scarf
Diagram Row 1: Work Square A, then Triangle B.
Diagram Row 2: Work Square A, Square C, Square D and Triangle B.
Diagram Row 3: Work Triangle E, Square D 3 times, and Triangle B.

Work Diagram Rows 4-10, as shown.

Work Diagram Rows 1-10 again to make second half of scarf.

Finishing
Weave in ends. Sew the two halves together as shown. Block gently to finished measurements.

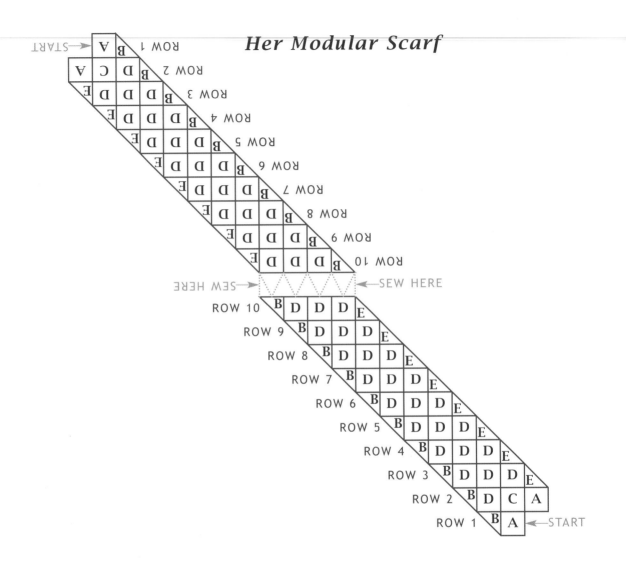

Her Modular Scarf

The Modules

Square A

CO 35 sts. Mark center stitch with a split marker or safety pin.

Row 1 (WS): Sl 1, K to end of row.
Row 2 (RS): Sl 1, K to 1 st before center st, dbl dec, K to end of row.

Repeat rows 1 and 2 until 3 sts remain.

Next row (WS): Sl 3.
Next row (RS): Dbl dec—1 st remains.

Triangle B

Start with one st on needle from just-finished square. Pick up and knit 17 sts along left side of just finished square—18 sts.

Row 1 (WS): Sl 1, K to end of row.
Row 2 (RS): Sl 1, K to last 2 sts, K2tog.

Repeat rows 1 and 2 until 2 sts remain.

Next row: K2tog. Fasten off.

Square C

Start with one st on needle from just-finished square. Pick up and knit 17 sts along left side of just finished square, and 17 sts along right side of next square—35 sts. Mark center stitch with a split marker or safety pin.

Row 1 (WS): Sl 1, K to end of row.
Row 2 (RS): Sl 1, K to 1 st before center st, dbl dec, K to end of row.

Repeat rows 1 and 2 until 3 sts remain.

Next row (WS): Sl 3.
Next row (RS): Dbl dec—1 st remains.

Square D

Start with one st on needle from just-finished square. Pick up and knit 16 sts along left side of just finished square, one st in corner, and 17 sts along right side of next square—35 sts. Mark center stitch with a split marker or safety pin.

Row 1 (WS): Sl 1, K to end of row.
Row 2 (RS): Sl 1, K to 1 st before center st, dbl dec, K to end of row.

Repeat rows 1 and 2 until 3 sts remain.

Next row (WS): Sl 3.
Next row (RS): Dbl dec—1 st remains.

Triangle E

Pick up and knit 18 sts along right side of first square in previous row.

Row 1 (WS): Sl 1, K to last 2 sts, K2tog.
Row 2 (RS): Sl 1, K to end of row.

Repeat rows 1 and 2 until 2 sts remain.

Next row: K2tog—1 st remains.

TIP

You will have ends to weave in at the beginning and end of each row of squares. Work them neatly into the same color so the back of your scarf looks as good as the front.

His Striped Scarf

Whether he favors a denim jacket, black leather, or a classic trench coat, this scarf is a perfect accent. With its conservative styling and masculine colors, any man would be pleased to wear it.

DIFFICULTY EASY

YARN LANA GROSSA FUN AND STRIPES (200 GRAMS)

NEEDLES 16" CIRCULAR US 3 (3.25 MM) *OR THE SIZE YOU NEED TO GET GAUGE*

MEASUREMENTS 8" X 56" (EXCLUDING FRINGE)

GAUGE 24 STS AND 32 ROWS = 4" IN STOCKINETTE STITCH

Scarf
CO 100 sts. Join into a circle, being careful not to twist your sts. Knit every round. Work until piece measures 56" long. BO. Sew ends of tube closed. Attach fringe if desired.

Fringe
Cut 200 strands 8" long. Tie groups of 4 strands at every other stitch along both ends of scarf. For the look shown, arrange your fringe so that all the strands in a group are the same color.

TIP
If you are going to fringe your scarf, cut the fringe first. That way you can just knit until you have just enough to bind off (about 2 yards).

Gloves & Mittens

Gloves & Mittens

Gloves & Mittens

Gloves & Mittens

Gloves & Mittens

Gloves & Mittens

Gloves & Mittens

Gloves

DIFFICULTY INTERMEDIATE

YARN LANA GROSSA MEILENWEIT FANTASY (100 GRAMS)

NEEDLES SET OF FOUR DOUBLE-POINTED US 1 (2.25 MM) *OR THE SIZE YOU NEED TO GET GAUGE*

SIZE WOMEN'S MEDIUM
MEASUREMENTS 8" HAND CIRCUMFERENCE AROUND PALM ABOVE THUMB

GAUGE 32 STS AND 44 ROWS = 4" IN STOCKINETTE STITCH

These fun, colorful gloves will brighten up your winter outerwear wardrobe. These are worked at a tight gauge on small needles for greater warmth and longer wear.

Cuff

Loosely CO 64 sts. Divide sts on three needles and join into a circle, being careful not to twist your sts. Work in K2 P2 ribbing for 2½".

Lower Palm

Set up round: K32, pm, m1, pm, K32.

Increase round: K to marker, sl marker, m1, K to marker, m1, sl marker, K to end of round.

Continue in St St, working increase round every 3rd round 10 times—21 sts between markers, 85 sts total.

Next round: K to marker, remove marker, place gusset sts on waste yarn for holding, remove marker, CO 1 st to bridge the gap, K to end of round—65 sts. Work even until palm measures 3¾" above ribbing.

Tip

Finger lengths vary quite a bit. If possible, have the intended wearer try on the gloves before finishing the fingers.

Little Finger

K8, place next 50 sts on waste yarn, CO 2 sts to bridge the gap, K to end of round—17 sts. Arrange sts evenly on 3 needles and work until little finger measures 2¼" long. Decrease and finish tip: K2tog 7 times, K3tog. Break yarn and thread through remaining 8 sts. Pull tight and fasten off.

Upper Palm

Place held sts on needles and join yarn at the base of the little finger. Pick up 2 sts along CO edge at base of little finger—52 sts. Work in stockinette stitch for 4 rounds.

Ring Finger

K9, place next 34 sts on waste yarn, CO 2 sts to bridge the gap, K9—20 sts. Arrange sts evenly on 3 needles and work until ring finger measures 2¾". Decrease and finish tip: K2tog 10 times, K2tog 5 times. Break yarn

and thread through remaining 5 sts. Pull tight and fasten off.

Middle Finger

Place held sts on needles and join yarn at the base of ring finger. K8, place next 18 sts on waste yarn, CO 2 sts to bridge the gap, K8, pick up 2 sts along CO edge at base of ring finger—20 sts.

Tip

It's fun to play with color on the fingers. Make them all the same, or make each finger different. You can wind off some yarn to get to just the section of the color sequence you want to use.

Arrange sts evenly on 3 needles and work until middle finger measures 3". Decrease and finish tip as for ring finger.

Index Finger

Place remaining sts on needles. Join yarn and pick up 2 sts along CO edge at base of middle finger—20 sts. Arrange sts evenly on 3 needles and work until index finger measures 2¾". Decrease and finish tip as for ring finger.

Thumb

Place held gusset sts on needles. Join yarn and pick up 1 st at palm—22 sts. Arrange sts evenly on 3 needles and work until thumb measures 2". K2tog 11 times. K2tog 4 times, K3tog. Break yarn and thread through remaining 5 sts. Pull tight and fasten off.

Finishing

Weave in ends and block to finished measurements.

Tip

Leave a generous tail when joining yarn at the beginning of each finger. When you weave in these tails, use them to close up any little gaps that develop at the base of the fingers.

Gauntlets

DIFFICULTY INTERMEDIATE

YARN LANA GROSSA MEILENWEIT FUN AND STRIPES (100 GRAMS)

NEEDLES SET OF FOUR DOUBLE-POINTED US 1 (2.25 MM) AND US 2 (2.75 MM) *OR THE SIZE YOU NEED TO GET GAUGE*

SIZE WOMEN'S MEDIUM
MEASUREMENTS 8" HAND CIRCUMFERENCE AROUND PALM ABOVE THUMB; LENGTH: 13"

GAUGE 30 STS AND 40 ROWS = 4" IN STOCKINETTE STITCH

Here's a kicky accent for your wardrobe. The Swirl Stitch pattern gives a lot of impact for surprisingly little effort. These gauntlets look far more difficult to knit than they are.

Swirl Stitch
Multiple of 6 sts.
Every Round: * K2, yo, K2, K2tog, repeat from * to end of round.

Garter Stitch
Round 1: K.
Round 2: P.
Repeat these two rounds.

Using size 2 needles, loosely CO 72 sts. Divide sts on three needles and join into a circle, being careful not to twist your sts. Work in Garter Stitch for 6 rounds.

Change to Swirl Stitch and work until piece measures 8½" from beginning.

Dec for hand
* K4, K2tog, repeat from * to end of round—60 sts.

Next round: Mark thumb gusset: K30, pm, m1, pm, K30.

Increase round: K to marker, sl marker, m1, K to marker, m1, sl marker, K to end of round.

Continue in st st, working increase round every third round until there are 19 sts in thumb gusset.

Next round: K to marker, remove marker, place gusset sts on waste yarn for holding, CO 1 st to bridge the gap, remove marker, K to end of round.

Continue without shaping for ½".

Change to size 1 needles and work in Garter Stitch for 6 rounds. BO loosely.

Place held gusset sts on size 1 needles. Join yarn and pick up 1 st at palm—20 sts. Arrange sts on 3 needles and work in Garter Stitch for 6 rounds. BO loosely.

Finishing
Weave in ends and block to finished measurements.

TIP
If you're careful to start both gauntlets at the same point in the color sequence, you need not count rows or pull out your tape measure to match the arm length. Just count repeats of the stripe sequence.

Fingerless Gloves

DIFFICULTY INTERMEDIATE

YARN LANA GROSSA MEILENWEIT COTTON MULTIRINGEL (100 GRAMS)

NEEDLES SET OF FOUR DOUBLE-POINTED US 1 (2.25 MM) *OR THE SIZE YOU NEED TO GET GAUGE*

SIZE WOMEN'S MEDIUM
MEASUREMENTS 8" HAND CIRCUMFERENCE AROUND PALM ABOVE THUMB

GAUGE 32 STS AND 44 ROWS = 4" IN STOCKINETTE STITCH

Leave your fingertips free for knitting or the keyboard—or just to show off a fresh manicure. The ruffled cuff makes these little gloves extra flirty. For a more tailored option, try the ribbed cuff.

Ruffled Cuff Pattern

Rounds 1 and 2: K.

Round 3: * K2tog 3 times, (yo, K1) 6 times, K2tog 3 times, repeat from * to end of round.

Round 4: P.

Seed Stitch

Round 1: * K1, P1, repeat from * to end of round.

Round 2: K the purl sts and P the knit sts as they face you.

Ruffled Cuff

CO 126 sts. Divide sts on three needles and join into a circle, being careful not to twist your sts.

Round 1: P.

Round 2: K.

Round 3: P.

Rounds 4-15: Work the four rounds of the Ruffled Cuff Pattern three times.

Round 16: K.

Decrease round: K2, * K2tog, repeat from * to end of round—64 sts.

Work in K2 P2 ribbing for 6 rounds. Continue with Lower Palm instructions.

Ribbed Cuff

Loosely CO 64 sts. Divide sts on three needles and join into a circle, being careful not to twist your sts. Work in K2 P2 ribbing until piece measures 3" from beginning. Continue with Lower Palm instructions.

Lower Palm

Set up round: K32, pm, m1, pm, K32.

Increase round: K to marker, sl marker, m1, K to marker, m1, sl marker, K to end of round.

Continue in st st, working increase round every 3rd round 10 times—21 sts between markers, 85 sts total.

Next round: K to marker, remove marker, place gusset sts on waste yarn for holding, remove marker, CO 1 st to bridge the gap, K to end of round—65 sts.

Work even until palm measures 3¾" above ribbing.

Little Finger

K8, place next 50 sts on waste yarn, CO 2 sts to bridge the gap, K to end of round—17 sts. Arrange sts evenly on 3 needles and work until little finger measures 1" long. Work 3 rounds in Seed Stitch. BO loosely in Seed Stitch.

Upper Palm

Place held sts on needles and join yarn at the base of the little finger. Pick up 2 sts along CO edge at base of little finger—52 sts. Work in st st for 4 rounds.

Ring Finger

K9, place next 34 sts on waste yarn, CO 2 sts to bridge the gap, K9—20 sts. Arrange sts evenly on 3 needles and work until ring finger measures 1½". Work 3 rounds in Seed Stitch. BO loosely in Seed Stitch.

Middle Finger

Place held sts on needles and join yarn at the base of ring finger. K8, place next 18 sts on waste yarn, CO 2 sts to bridge the gap, K8, pick up 2 sts along CO edge at base of ring finger—20 sts. Arrange sts evenly on 3 needles and work until middle finger measures 1¾". Work 3 rounds in Seed Stitch. BO loosely in Seed Stitch.

TIP

Leave a generous tail when joining yarn at the beginning of each finger. When you weave in these tails, use them to close up any little gaps that develop at the base of the fingers.

Index Finger

Place remaining sts on needles. Join yarn and pick up 2 sts along CO edge at base of middle finger—20 sts. Arrange sts evenly on 3 needles and work until index finger measures 1½". Work 3 rounds in Seed Stitch. BO loosely in Seed Stitch.

Thumb

Place held gusset sts on needles. Join yarn and pick up 1 st at palm—22 sts. Arrange sts evenly on 3 needles and work until thumb measures 1". Work 3 rounds in Seed Stitch. BO loosely in Seed Stitch.

Finishing

Weave in ends and block to finished measurements.

Make the ribbed cuff version for your favorite man to keep his hands warm for all those winter chores...

Mittens

DIFFICULTY INTERMEDIATE

YARN LANA GROSSA MEILENWEIT MULTIRINGEL (100 GRAMS)

NEEDLES SET OF FOUR DOUBLE-POINTED US 1 (2.25 MM) *OR THE SIZE YOU NEED TO GET GAUGE*

SIZE X-SMALL (SMALL, MEDIUM, LARGE)
MEASUREMENT 6" (7", 8", 9") HAND CIRCUMFERENCE AROUND PALM ABOVE THUMB

GAUGE 32 STS AND 44 ROWS = 4" IN STOCKINETTE STITCH

TIP

When finishing off the tip of your mitten or glove fingers, run the end of the yarn through the final few stitches twice, then pull tight. Two strands will fill the stitches more completely and give a better-looking result.

Cuff

Loosely CO 48 (56, 64, 72) sts. Divide sts on three needles and join into a circle, being careful not to twist your sts. Knit 8 rounds for rolled edge. Work in K2 P2 ribbing for 2¾". Change to st st and work one round.

Lower Palm

Set-up round: K24 (28, 32, 36), pm, m1, pm, K24 (28, 32, 36).

Increase round: K to marker, sl marker, m1, K to marker, m1, sl marker, K to end of round.

Continue in st st, working increase round every 3rd round 8 (9, 10, 12) times—17 (19, 21, 25) sts between markers, 65 (75, 85, 97) sts total.

Next round: K to marker, remove marker, place gusset sts on waste yarn for holding, remove marker, CO 1 st to bridge the gap, K to end of round—49 (57, 65, 73) sts.

Work even until palm measures 3½" (4½", 5½", 6½") above ribbing, decreasing 1 st on last row.

Shape Top

Round 1: * K10 (12, 14, 16), K2tog, repeat from * 3 times more—44 (52, 60, 68) sts.
Round 2: K.

Repeat these two rounds, working one less st between decreases and decreasing 4 sts every other round, until 24 (28, 32, 36) sts remain. Then discontinue plain rounds and decrease 4 sts every round until 8 sts remain. Break yarn, draw through remaining 8 sts, pull tight and fasten off.

Thumb

Place held gusset sts on needles. Join yarn and pick up 1 st at palm—18 (20, 22, 26) sts. Arrange sts evenly on 3 needles and work until thumb measures 1" (1¼", 1¾", 2"). K2tog 9 (10, 11, 13) times. K2tog 3 (5, 4, 5) times, K3tog 1 (0, 1, 1) time. Break yarn and thread through remaining 4 (5, 5, 6) sts. Pull tight and fasten off.

Finishing

Weave in ends and block to finished measurements.

Here's the classic winter hand warmer with a rolled edge on the cuff. Make these mittens for the whole family. Let the stripes fall where they may!

Dog Sweater

Dog Sweater

Dog Sweater

Dog Sweater

Dog Sweater

Dog Sweater

Dog Sweater

Dog Sweater

Your dog will be the envy of all her buddies at the park when she shows up in this stylish sweater. If you really want to set the park abuzz, make the matching wristlets!

Back

Using circular needle, CO 84 sts. Work in st st in rows until piece measures 15". BO.

Chest

Using circular needle, CO 30 sts. Work in st st in rows until piece measures 8". Continuing in st st, dec 1 st at each end of every 4th row 11 times—8 sts. Work even until piece measures 12". BO.

Sew chest piece to back 5" from lower edge and 4" from neck edge, leaving 3" openings for legs as shown in the schematic.

Neckband

Using double pointed needles, pick up and knit 100 sts around neck edge. Work K2 P2 ribbing for 1". BO loosely.

Lower Edge

Using circular needle, pick up and knit 120 sts around lower edge. Work K2 P2 ribbing for 1". BO loosely.

Leg Bands

Using double pointed needles, pick up and knit 44 sts around each leg opening. Work K2 P2 ribbing for 1". BO loosely.

Finishing

Weave in ends. Block to finished measurements.

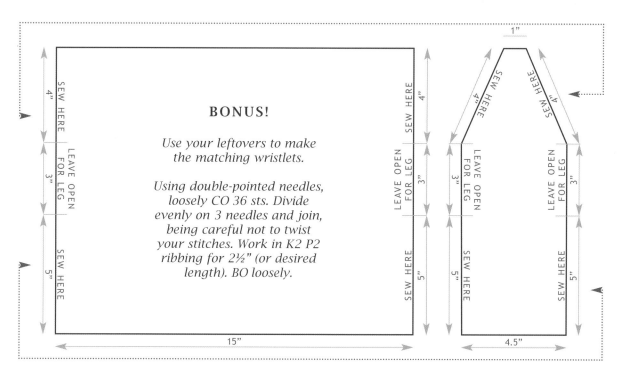

BONUS!

Use your leftovers to make the matching wristlets.

Using double-pointed needles, loosely CO 36 sts. Divide evenly on 3 needles and join, being careful not to twist your stitches. Work in K2 P2 ribbing for 2½" (or desired length). BO loosely.

Socks & Leg Warmers

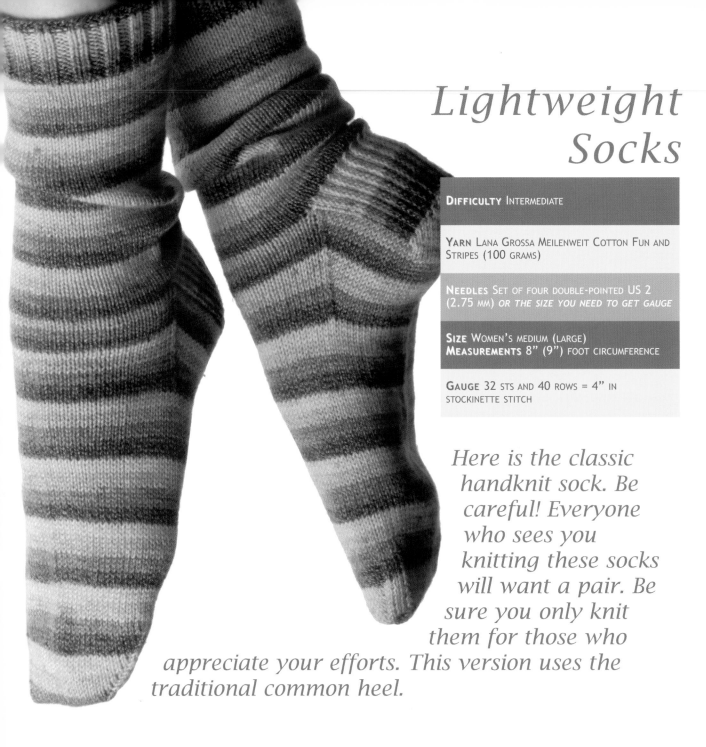

Lightweight Socks

DIFFICULTY INTERMEDIATE

YARN LANA GROSSA MEILENWEIT COTTON FUN AND STRIPES (100 GRAMS)

NEEDLES SET OF FOUR DOUBLE-POINTED US 2 (2.75 MM) *OR THE SIZE YOU NEED TO GET GAUGE*

SIZE WOMEN'S MEDIUM (LARGE)
MEASUREMENTS 8" (9") FOOT CIRCUMFERENCE

GAUGE 32 STS AND 40 ROWS = 4" IN STOCKINETTE STITCH

Here is the classic handknit sock. Be careful! Everyone who sees you knitting these socks will want a pair. Be sure you only knit them for those who appreciate your efforts. This version uses the traditional common heel.

Cuff
Loosely CO 64 (72) sts. Arrange evenly on three needles and join into a circle, being careful not to twist your sts. Work in K2 P2 ribbing for 2".

Leg
Change to st st and work until piece measures 8" from cast on edge.

Divide for Heel
K16 (18) sts. Sl remaining sts on this needle to needle 2 for holding. Turn work. Sl 1, P31 (35). Move remaining sts on this needle to needle 2 for holding. You now have 32 (36) sts held on needle 2 for your instep, and 32 (36) sts to work for your heel flap.

Heel Flap (worked back and forth in rows)
Row 1 (RS): * Sl 1, K1, repeat from * to end of row.
Row 2: Sl 1, P to end of row.

Repeat these two rows 14 (16) times more, then work row 1 again—31 (35) rows.

Turn Heel
Row 1: Sl 1, P16 (18), P2tog, P1, turn.
Row 2: Sl 1, K3, K2tog, K1, turn.
Row 3: Sl 1, P4, P2tog, P1, turn.
Row 4: Sl 1, K5, K2tog, K1, turn.
Row 5: Sl 1, P6, P2tog, P1, turn.
Row 6: Sl 1, K7, K2tog, K1, turn.
Row 7: Sl 1, P8, P2tog, P1, turn.
Row 8: Sl 1, K9, K2tog, K1, turn.
Row 9: Sl 1, P10, P2tog, P1, turn.
Row 10: Sl 1, K11, K2tog, K1, turn.
Row 11: Sl 1, P12, P2tog, P1, turn.
Row 12: Sl 1, K13, K2tog, K1, turn.
Row 13: Sl 1, P14, P2tog, P1, turn.
Row 14: Sl 1, K15, K2tog, K1. For first size, 18 sts remain. Go to *Pick up Sts for Gussets*. For second size, continue with rows 15 and 16.
Row 15: Sl 1, P16, P2tog, P1, turn.
Row 16: Sl 1, K17, K2tog, K1—20 sts remain.

Pick up Sts for Gussets
Continuing with the needle holding your heel sts, pick up and knit 16 (18) sts down the left side of heel flap. Using a second needle, K32 (36) sts at instep. Using a third needle, pick up and knit 16 (18) sts up the right side of heel flap. K9 (10) sts to center of heel. 82 (92) sts. Beg of round is at center of heel. K one round.

Decrease Gussets
Round 1:
Needle 1—K to last 3 sts, K2tog, K1.
Needle 2—K.
Needle 3—K1, SSK, K to end of round.
Round 2: K.

Alternate these two rounds 8 (9) times more—64 (72) sts.

Foot
Continue without shaping until foot is 2" less then desired foot length measured from back of heel (about 8" for a women's shoe size 8).

Shape Toe
Round 1:
Needle 1—K to last 3 sts, K2tog, K1.
Needle 2—K1, SSK, K to last 3 sts, K2tog, K1.
Needle 3—K1, SSK, K to end of round.
Round 2: K.

Repeat these 2 rounds 7 (8) times more—32 (36) sts.

K sts on needle 1 so that yarn is coming out the side of the toe.

Finishing
Graft toe closed with kitchener stitch.

Thicker Socks

DIFFICULTY INTERMEDIATE

YARN LANA GROSSA MEILENWEIT 6 FACH MULTI JACQUARD (100 GRAMS)

NEEDLES SET OF FOUR DOUBLE-POINTED US 3 (3.25 MM) *OR THE SIZE YOU NEED TO GET GAUGE*

SIZE WOMEN'S MEDIUM
MEASUREMENTS 8" FOOT CIRCUMFERENCE

GAUGE 24 STS AND 32 ROWS TO 4" IN STOCKINETTE STITCH

If you like your socks a little thicker, or just don't want to work with size 1 or 2 needles, here's the sock in a heavier, 6-ply yarn. This version uses the traditional common heel.

Cuff

Loosely CO 48 sts. Arrange so that you have 16 sts on each needle and join into a circle, being careful not to twist your sts. Work in K2 P2 ribbing for 2".

Leg

Change to st st and work until piece measures 8" from cast on edge.

Divide for Heel

K12 sts. Sl 4 sts remaining on this needle to needle 2 for holding. Turn work. Sl 1, P23. Move 4 sts remaining on this needle to needle 2 for holding. You now have 24 sts held on needle 2 for your instep, and 24 sts to work for your heel flap.

Heel Flap (worked back and forth in rows)

Row 1 (RS): * Sl 1, K1, repeat from * to end of row.
Row 2: Sl 1, P to end of row.

Repeat these two rows 10 times more, then work row 1 again—23 rows.

> **TIP**
> *When you count rows on your heel flap, the slipped stitches will be bigger, and therefore easier to count. Each slipped stitch counts as 2 rows.*

Turn Heel

Row 1: Sl 1, P12, P2tog, P1, turn.
Row 2: Sl 1, K3, K2tog, K1, turn.
Row 3: Sl 1, P4, P2tog, P1, turn.
Row 4: Sl 1, K5, K2tog, K1, turn.
Row 5: Sl 1, P6, P2tog, P1, turn.
Row 6: Sl 1, K7, K2tog, K1, turn.
Row 7: Sl 1, P8, P2tog, P1, turn.
Row 8: Sl 1, K9, K2tog, K1, turn.
Row 9: Sl 1, P10, P2tog, P1, turn.
Row 10: Sl 1, K11, K2tog, K1—14 sts.

Pick up Sts for Gussets

Continuing with the needle holding your heel sts, pick up and knit 12 sts down the left side of heel flap. Using a second needle, K24 sts at instep. Using a third needle, pick up and knit 12 sts up the right side of heel flap. K7 sts to center of heel—62 sts. Beg of round is at center of heel. K one round.

Decrease Gussets

Round 1:
Needle 1—K to last 3 sts, K2tog, K1.
Needle 2—K.
Needle 3—K1, SSK, K to end of round.
Round 2: K.

Alternate these two rounds 6 times more—48 sts.

Foot

Continue without shaping until foot is 2" less then desired foot length measured from back of heel (about 8" for a women's shoe size 8).

Shape Toe

Round 1:
Needle 1—K to last 3 sts, K2tog, K1.
Needle 2—K1, SSK, K to last 3 sts, K2tog, K1.
Needle 3—K1, SSK, K to end of round.
Round 2: K.

Repeat these 2 rounds 5 times more—24 sts.

Knit sts on needle 1 so that yarn is coming out side of toe.

Finishing

Graft toe closed with kitchener stitch.

Cuff

Loosely CO 104 sts. Arrange evenly on three needles and join into a circle, being careful not to twist your sts. Work in K2 P2 ribbing for 2".

Leg

Change to st st and work until piece measures 9" from cast on edge.

Decrease round: K1, K2tog, K to last 3 sts, SSK, K1.

Continue in st st, working decrease round every third round 12 times—80 sts. Continue without shaping until piece measures 13" from beginning.

Work in K2 P2 ribbing for 2".

BO loosely.

Finishing

Weave in ends. Block to finished measurements.

Leg Warmers

DIFFICULTY EASY

YARN LANA GROSSA MULTIRINGEL (150 GRAMS)

NEEDLES SET OF FOUR DOUBLE-POINTED US 2 (2.75 MM) *OR THE SIZE YOU NEED TO GET GAUGE*

SIZE WOMEN'S MEDIUM
MEASUREMENTS 13" CIRCUMFERENCE AT CALF AND 15" LONG

GAUGE 32 STS AND 40 ROWS TO 4" IN STOCKINETTE STITCH

Not just a Flashdance flashback, leg warmers are an enduring favorite with skaters and dancers.

Bull's Eye Heel Socks

These socks feature a different kind of heel. Sometimes called a Turkish Heel or Afterthought Heel, this style creates a fun bull's eye effect when worked with self-striping yarns. It has the added benefit of being easy to take out and re-knit if you develop a hole in the heel.

DIFFICULTY INTERMEDIATE

YARN LANA GROSSA MEILENWEIT JACQUARD (100 GRAMS)

NEEDLES SET OF FOUR DOUBLE-POINTED US 2 (2.75 MM) OR *THE SIZE YOU NEED TO GET GAUGE*

SIZE WOMEN'S MEDIUM (LARGE)
MEASUREMENTS 8" (9") FOOT CIRCUMFERENCE

GAUGE 32 STS AND 40 ROWS TO 4" IN STOCKINETTE STITCH

Cuff
Loosely CO 64 (72) sts. Arrange evenly on three needles and join into a circle, being careful not to twist your sts. Work in K2 P2 ribbing for 2".

Leg
Change to st st and work until piece measures 8" from cast on edge.

Reserve Stitches for Heel
Using waste yarn, K32 (36) sts. Turn and P the same 32 (36) sts. Drop waste yarn.

Foot
Continue with main yarn in st st until 6" (7") past waste yarn. Here is where you adjust for foot length—you should work until the portion after the waste yarn measures 4" less than your foot from back of heel to tip of toe.

TIP
Use a smooth yarn of contrasting color for your waste yarn. You will then be able to pull it out easily without leaving fuzz behind. Your waste yarn should be the same or slightly thinner than your sock yarn.

Shape Toe
Round 1: K1, SSK, K26 (30), K2tog, K2, SSK, K26 (30) K2tog, K1.
Round 2 and all even numbered rounds: K.
Round 3: K1, SSK, K24 (28), K2tog, K2, SSK, K24 (28) K2tog, K1.
Round 5: K1, SSK, K22 (26), K2tog, K2, SSK, K22 (26) K2tog, K1.
Round 7: K1, SSK, K20 (24), K2tog, K2, SSK, K20 (24) K2tog, K1.
Round 9: K1, SSK, K18 (22), K2tog, K2, SSK, K18 (22) K2tog, K1.
Round 11: K1, SSK, K16 (20), K2tog, K2, SSK, K16 (20) K2tog, K1.
Round 13: K1, SSK, K14 (18), K2tog, K2, SSK, K14 (18) K2tog, K1.
Round 15: K1, SSK, K12 (16), K2tog, K2, SSK, K12 (16) K2tog, K1.
Round 17 (larger size only): K1, SSK, K14, K2tog, K2, SSK, K14, K2tog, K1.

Arrange sts evenly on two needles with working yarn at the side of the toe.

Graft toe closed with kitchener stitch.

Shape Heel
Remove waste yarn, recovering 32 (36) sts at each side of opening. Arrange sts on 3 needles, join yarn at side of opening, and K 1 round.

Shape and close the heel just as you did the toe.

Finishing
Weave in ends and block to finished measurements.

Thicker Bull's Eye Heel Socks

Here's the Bull's Eye Heel Sock with a thicker yarn. This is a great look for those of you who like to wear socks with your Birkenstocks!

DIFFICULTY INTERMEDIATE

YARN LANA GROSSA MEILENWEIT 6 FACH MULTI JACQUARD (100 GRAMS)

NEEDLES SET OF FOUR DOUBLE-POINTED US 3 (3.25 MM) OR THE SIZE YOU NEED TO GET GAUGE

SIZE WOMEN'S MEDIUM (LARGE)
MEASUREMENTS 8" (9") FOOT CIRCUMFERENCE

GAUGE 24 STS AND 23 ROWS = 4" IN STOCKINETTE STITCH

Cuff

Loosely CO 48 (56) sts. Arrange evenly on three needles and join into a circle, being careful not to twist your sts. Work in K2 P2 ribbing for 2".

Leg

Change to st st and work until piece measures 8" from cast on edge.

Reserve Stitches for Heel

Using waste yarn, K24 (28) sts. Turn and P the same 24 (28) sts. Drop waste yarn.

Foot

Continue with main yarn in st st until 6" (7") past waste yarn. Here is where you adjust for foot length—you should work until the portion after the waste yarn measures 4" less than your foot from back of heel to tip of toe.

Shape Toe

Round 1: K1, SSK, K18 (22), K2tog, K2, SSK, K18 (22) K2tog, K1.
Round 2 and all even numbered rounds: K.

TIP

To recover sts from waste yarn, use a needle one size smaller than your working needles. Slide the tip of this needle under the right hand leg of each st. When all sts are on the needle, pick out the waste yarn. Knit the sts on to the correct size needle when working the first row.

Round 3: K1, SSK, K16 (20), K2tog, K2, SSK, K16 (20) K2tog, K1.
Round 5: K1, SSK, K14 (18), K2tog, K2, SSK, K14 (18) K2tog, K1.
Round 7: K1, SSK, K12 (16), K2tog, K2, SSK, K12 (16) K2tog, K1.
Round 9: K1, SSK, K10 (14), K2tog, K2, SSK, K10 (14) K2tog, K1.
Round 11: K1, SSK, K8 (12), K2tog, K2, SSK, K8 (12) K2tog, K1.
Round 13 (larger size only): K1, SSK, K10, K2tog, K2, SSK, K10, K2tog, K1.

Arrange sts evenly on two needles with working yarn at the side of the toe.

Graft toe closed with kitchener stitch.

Shape Heel

Remove waste yarn, recovering 24 (28) sts at each side of opening. Arrange sts on 3 needles, join yarn at side of opening, and K 1 round. Shape and close the heel just as you did the toe.

Finishing

Weave in ends and block to finished measurements.

Hats

Hats

Hats

Hats

Hats

Hats

Hats

DIFFICULTY EASY

YARN LANA GROSSA MEILENWEIT 6 FACH FUN AND STRIPES (100 GRAMS)

NEEDLES 16" CIRCULAR AND SET OF FOUR DOUBLE-POINTED US 4 (3.50 MM) *OR THE SIZE YOU NEED TO GET GAUGE*

SIZE ADULT SMALL (LARGE)
MEASUREMENTS 20" (22") CIRCUMFERENCE

GAUGE 24 STS AND 23 ROWS = 4" IN K2 P2 RIBBING, SLIGHTLY STRETCHED

Skater Beanie

When the teenage boy in your life agrees to let you knit him a hat, this is what he has in mind. This is a classic watch cap to keep in a coat pocket for cold evenings.

Using circular needle, CO 120 (132) sts. Join into a circle, being careful not to twist your sts. Work in K2 P2 ribbing until piece measures 8" from beginning.

Shape Crown
Change to double-pointed needles when necessary.
Round 1: * (K2, P2) 2 times, K2, P2tog, repeat from * to end of round.
Round 2: * K2, P2, K2, P2tog, K2, P1, repeat from * to end of round.
Round 3: * K2, P2tog, (K2, P1) 2 times, repeat from * to end of round.
Round 4: * (K2, P1) 2 times, K2tog, P1, repeat from * to end of round.
Round 5: * K2, P1, K2tog, P1, K1, P1, repeat from * to end of round
Round 6: * K2tog, P1, (K1, P1) 2 times, repeat from * to end of round.
Round 7: * (K1, P1) 2 times, SSK, repeat from * to end of round.
Round 8: * K1, P1, SSK, K1, repeat from * to end of round.
Round 9: * SSK, K2, repeat from * to end of round.
Round 10: * K1, K2tog, repeat from * to end of round.
Round 11: * K2tog, repeat from * to end of round

Break yarn, draw through remaining 10 sts, pull tight and fasten off.

Finishing
Weave in ends.

Sideways Hat

This little hat turns the stripes on their side for a fun look.

DIFFICULTY INTERMEDIATE

YARN LANA GROSSA MEILENWEIT MULTIEFFEKT (50 GRAMS)

NEEDLES 16" CIRCULAR AND SET OF FOUR DOUBLE-POINTED US 2 (2.75 MM) *OR THE SIZE YOU NEED TO GET GAUGE*

SIZE ADULT MEDIUM
MEASUREMENTS 21" CIRCUMFERENCE

GAUGE 28 STS AND 36 ROWS = 4" IN STOCKINETTE STITCH

Body of Hat
Using circular needle and waste yarn, CO 36 sts. Change to main yarn and work in st st in rows until piece measures 21". Remove waste yarn. As you pick out the waste yarn stitch by stitch, you will free the bottom loops of your first row of knitting. Place these new sts on one of your double-pointed needles. Graft the ends of your strip together using kitchener stitch.

Brim
Using 16" circular needle, pick up 128 sts evenly along edge of strip (about 2 sts for every 3 rows). P 1 round. K 1 round. Repeat these 2 rounds 2 times more—3 ridges made. BO loosely in purl.

Crown
Using 16" circular needle, pick up 128 sts evenly along edge of strip (about 2 sts for every 3 rows). P 1 round. K 1 round. Repeat these 2 rounds 3 times more—4 ridges made.

Decrease for Top of Hat
Round 1: * K14, K2tog, repeat from * to end of round.
Round 2 and all even numbered rounds: K.

Round 3: * K13, K2tog, repeat from * to end of round.
Round 5: * K12, K2tog, repeat from * to end of round.
Round 7: * K11, K2tog, repeat from * to end of round.
Round 9: * K10, K2tog, repeat from * to end of round.

Change to double-pointed needles.

Round 11: * K9, K2tog, repeat from * to end of round.
Round 13: * K8, K2tog, repeat from * to end of round.
Round 15: * K7, K2tog, repeat from * to end of round.
Round 17: * K6, K2tog, repeat from * to end of round.
Round 19: * K5, K2tog, repeat from * to end of round.
Round 21: * K4, K2tog, repeat from * to end of round.
Round 23: * K3, K2tog, repeat from * to end of round.
Round 25: * K2, K2tog, repeat from * to end of round.
Round 27: * K1, K2tog, repeat from * to end of round.
Round 28: * K2tog, repeat from * to end of round.

Break yarn, draw through remaining 8 sts, pull tight and fasten off.

Finishing
Weave in ends. Steam lightly to eliminate any curl at brim and to smooth out crown.

Stocking Cap

This classic pointed stocking cap looks vaguely Nordic. It is especially cute on children, or on skiers and snowboarders—the point will trail behind in the wind!

DIFFICULTY EASY

YARN LANA GROSSA MEILENWEIT MULTIEFFEKT (100 GRAMS)

NEEDLES 16" CIRCULAR AND SET OF FOUR DOUBLE-POINTED US 2 (2.75 MM) *OR THE SIZE YOU NEED TO GET GAUGE*

SIZE CHILD SMALL (CHILD LARGE, ADULT SMALL, ADULT LARGE)
MEASUREMENTS 16" (18", 20", 22") CIRCUMFERENCE

GAUGE 30 STS AND 36 ROWS = 4" IN STOCKINETTE STITCH

Using circular needle, CO 120 (136, 148, 164) sts. Join into a circle, being careful not to twist your sts. Purl 2 rounds. Work in K2 P2 ribbing for 6 rounds. Purl 2 rounds. Change to st st and work in rounds for 5" (6", 6½", 7").

Set Up for Crown Shaping
Next round: * K30 (34, 37, 41) sts, pm, repeat from * 3 times more.

Next round (decrease round): * K to 2 sts before marker, K2tog, slip marker, repeat from * 3 times more.

Continue in st st, working decrease round every third round and switching to double-pointed needles when necessary, until 4 sts remain.

Break yarn, draw through remaining 4 sts, pull tight and fasten off.

Finishing
Embellish your hat with a pompon or tassel at the point.

Weave in ends.

Drawstring Bag

Drawstring Bag

Drawstring Bag

Drawstring Bag

Drawstring Bag

Drawstring Bag

Drawstring Bag

Drawstring Bag

DIFFICULTY EASY

YARN LANA GROSSA MEILENWEIT MULTIRINGEL (100 GRAMS)

NEEDLES 16" CIRCULAR AND SET OF FOUR DOUBLE-POINTED US 2 (2.75 MM) *OR THE SIZE YOU NEED TO GET GAUGE*

SIZE 10" CIRCUMFERENCE, 6" TALL

GAUGE 32 STS AND 40 ROWS = 4" IN STOCKINETTE STITCH

This little bag will hold whatever you treasure, from magical talismans to the tiles for your Scrabble game.

Using circular needle, CO 240 sts. Join into a circle, being careful not to twist your sts.

Ruffle

Round 1: * K9, P3, repeat from * to end of round.
Round 2: Repeat round 1.
Round 3: * SSK, K5, K2tog, P3, repeat from * to end of round.
Round 4: * K7, P3, repeat from * to end of round.
Round 5: * SSK, K3, K2tog, P3, repeat from * to end of round.
Round 6: * K5, P3, repeat from * to end of round.
Round 7: * SSK, K1, K2tog, P3, repeat from * to end of round.
Round 8: * K3, P3, repeat from * to end of round.
Round 9: * Sl 1, K2tog, psso, P3, repeat from * to end of round.
Round 10: * K1, P3, repeat from * to end of round—80 sts.

Casing

Switch to double-pointed needles.

Rounds 1-3: K.

Round 4: * K2tog, yo, SSK, K36, repeat from * once more.

Round 5: * K1, (K1, P1) into yo of previous round, K38, (K1, P1) into yo of previous round, K37.

Rounds 6-12: K.

Turn the bag inside out. You are going to turn the work around and knit in the opposite direction, reversing the right side and wrong side of the work. This lets the right side of the bag lie under the right side of the ruffle.

Continue in st st until the piece measures 5" from end of casing.

Shape Bottom

Set up round: * K16, pm, repeat from * to end of round—5 markers placed.

Decrease round: * K to 2 sts before marker, K2tog, repeat from * to end of round.

Continue in st st, working decrease round every round until 10 sts remain. Break yarn and draw through remaining 10 sts. Pull tight and fasten off.

Fold casing in half with ruffle to outside of bag. Sew first row of casing to last row of casing, leaving ruffle free.

Make 2 twisted cords approximately 24" long. Thread first cord completely through casing, starting and ending through the same eyelet. Tie ends together. Thread the second cord completely through the casing, starting and ending through the other eyelet. Tie ends together.

TWISTED CORD

Cut about 4 yards of yarn. Fold the yarn in half and tie the ends together to make a loop. Have a buddy hold the knot, or loop it over a sturdy table leg. Insert a knitting needle at the fold and start twisting. Twist until you think you've done enough, then twist some more. The more you twist, the better your cord. Bring the fold to meet the knot, allowing the cord to twist back on itself. Tie the knot end and the fold end together. You should end up with a tidy rope.

Poncho & Vest

Poncho & Vest

Poncho & Vest

Poncho & Vest

Poncho & Vest

Poncho & Vest

Poncho & Vest

Vest

This lightweight vest is a colorful accent to layer over your wardrobe basics.

DIFFICULTY INTERMEDIATE

YARN LANA GROSSA MEILENWEIT MULTIEFFEKT (200 GRAMS)

NEEDLES 29" CIRCULAR US 3 (3.25 MM) OR THE SIZE YOU NEED TO GET GAUGE

MEASUREMENTS
CHEST 36" (40")
LENGTH 18" (18")

GAUGE 28 STS AND 36 ROWS = 4" IN STOCKINETTE STITCH

Note

Work the lower body in one piece, beginning at one front edge and working around to the other. Pick up sts from the side of the lower body piece to work the upper back and front sections.

Lower Body

CO 63 (63) sts. Work in st st until 36" (40") long. Measure along one side of this strip and place a marker in the knitting at 7", 11", 25" and 29" (8", 12", 28" and 32").

Back

With RS facing, pick up and knit 98 (112) sts between second and third markers. Work in st st until 9" from pick up.

> **TIP**
> *Don't panic when you see the edges of your vest curling up. This curl is perfectly normal for stockinette stitch. It will flatten out when you block your vest.*

Shape Shoulders

BO 8 (11) sts at beg of next 4 rows, then 9 (10) sts at beg of next 2 rows. BO rem 48 (48) sts.

Right Front

With RS facing, pick up and knit 49 (56) sts between front edge and first marker. Work in st st, decreasing 1 st at neck edge every 3rd row 24 times—25 (32) sts. Continue until same length as back to shoulder.

Shape Shoulders

BO 8 (11) sts at beg of next 2 WS rows. BO rem 9 (10) sts.

Left Front

With RS facing, pick up and knit 49 (56) sts between last marker and left front edge. Work in st st, decreasing 1 st at neck edge every 3rd row 24 times— 25 (32) sts. Continue until same length as back to shoulder.

Shape Shoulders

BO 8 (11) sts at beg of next 2 RS rows. BO rem 9 (10) sts. Sew fronts to back at shoulders.

Bottom, Front and Neck Edging

Beg at lower left front corner, with RS facing, pick up and knit 3 sts for every 4 rows along lower edge, 1 st for every st along lower right front edge, 3 sts for every 4 rows along upper right front edge, 1 st for every st along back neck edge, 3 sts for every 4 rows along upper left front edge, and 1 st for every st along lower left front edge. You may want to use a longer circular needle for this if you have one handy, but it is entirely possible to get all these sts on your 29" needle. It's OK to crowd them together.

Knitted Cord Edging

Starting with the first st you picked up, use cable cast on to add 4 sts. *K3, SSK, sl these 4 sts back to left hand needle, repeat from * all the way around. When 4 sts remain, BO and sew ends of edging together.

Armhole Edging

Beg at back corner, pick up and knit 3 sts for every 4 rows around armhole. Work knitted cord edging as above.

Ties

Make 2 knitted cords each 6" long. Sew to front edges where upper and lower fronts meet.

Knitted Cord

CO 4 sts. * K4, slide these 4 sts back to left hand needle, repeat from * until cord is desired length. BO

Finishing

Weave in ends. Block to finished measurements.

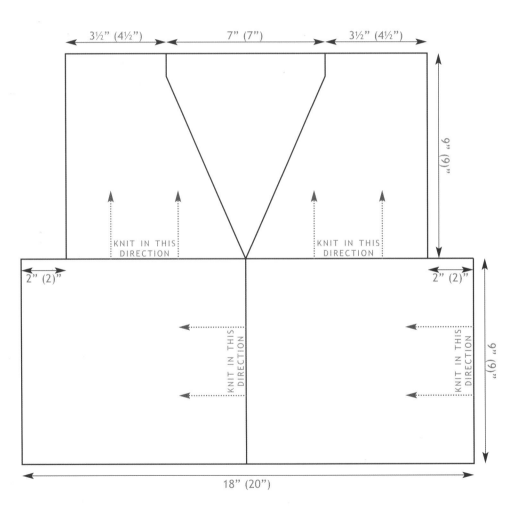

Poncho

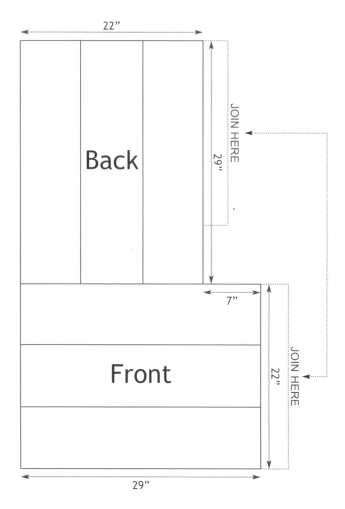

22"

Back

JOIN HERE

29"

7"

Front

JOIN HERE

22"

29"

DIFFICULTY INTERMEDIATE

YARN LANA GROSSA MEILENWEIT FANTASY (500 GRAMS)

NEEDLES TWO 24" CIRCULAR US 3 (3.25 MM) *OR THE SIZE YOU NEED TO GET GAUGE.* Size D crochet hook.

SIZE 33" LONG FROM NECK TO BOTTOM POINT

GAUGE 24 STS AND 32 ROWS = 4" IN STOCKINETTE STITCH

Carol Lapin designed this great poncho. Carol's selective use of speckled yarn to join the strips is a wonderful accent.

Note
This poncho is made up of 6 strips—3 for the front and 3 for the back.

Strips (make 6)
CO 46 sts. Work in st st until piece is 29" long. BO.

Assembly

Find the section of your yarn that is speckled. Use this section of yarn for all assembly, adding new lengths of yarn as needed. Join three strips together for the front panel and the other three strips for the back panel.

To join strips

With RS facing, pick up and knit 1 st for every row along side of first strip. Using the second circular needle, pick up and knit 1 st for every row along side of second strip. Work 3-needle bind off to join strips together. Attach the third strip in the same way.

Join Front Panel to Back Panel

Following diagram, pick up and knit one st for every st along the end of one panel. Pick up the same number of sts along the side of the other panel, leaving 7" free at the end. Work 3-needle bind off to join panels together. Repeat with other end.

Bottom Edge

Work 1 single crochet in each st around bottom of Poncho.

Round 2: Work 2 double crochets in each single crochet around.

Round 3: Work 1 double crochet in each double crochet around.

Neck Edge

Work 1 single crochet in each st around neck edge.

Round 2: Work 2 double crochets in each single crochet around.

Finishing

Weave in ends. Block to finished measurements.

A Gift Set for Baby

A Gift Set for Baby

A Gift Set for Baby

A Gift Set for Baby

A Gift Set for Baby

A Gift Set for Baby

A Gift Set for Baby

Sweater

BABY SWEATER
DIFFICULTY EASY

YARN LANA GROSSA MEILENWEIT FUN AND STRIPES
(100 GRAMS)

NEEDLES US 2 (2.75 MM) AND US 3 (3.25 MM)
OR SIZE YOU NEED TO GET GAUGE

NOTIONS STITCH HOLDERS; 3 (3, 4) 3/8"
BUTTONS

SIZES NEWBORN (6 MONTHS, 12 MONTHS)

CHEST 20" (22", 24")
LENGTH 7½" (8", 9")
SLEEVE LENGTH 6" (6½", 7")

GAUGE 26 STS AND 40 ROWS = 4" ON US 3 IN
GARTER RIB PATTERN

This is the gift that will make all the other guests at the baby shower jealous! Try a playful unisex colorway.

Border Pattern In Rows
Rows 1, 3 and 5 (WS): P.
Rows 2 and 4: K.
Rows 6 and 8: * K2, P2, repeat from * to end of row.
Rows 7 and 9: K the knit sts and P the purl sts as they face you.

Border Pattern In Rounds
Rounds 1-5: K.
Rounds 6-9: * K2, P2, repeat from * to end of round.

Garter Rib Pattern
Row or round 1 (RS): K.
Row or round 2: * K2, P2, repeat from * to end of row.

Edge Stitch

The first st of every row is slipped as if to purl, and the last st of every row is knit to create a tidy edge for seaming. The border and garter rib patterns are worked between these edge sts. The edge sts are included in the st counts given.

Back

With smaller needle, CO 66 (72, 78) sts. Work Border Pattern In Rows. Change to larger needles and work in Garter Rib Pattern until piece measures 7½" (8", 9"), ending with a RS row.

Shape Shoulders

BO first 20 (23, 26) sts on next row. Work next 26 sts in patt and place on st holder for back neck. Work in pattern to end of row. Change to smaller needles and work 8 rows of K2 P2 ribbing for button band. BO remaining 20 (23, 26) sts.

Front

Work as for back until piece measures 6" (6½", 7½"), ending with a WS row.

Shape Neck

Maintaining pattern as established, work 23 (26, 29) sts. Place remaining sts on holder. Working left front neck only, dec 1 st at neck edge every other row 3 times—20 (23, 26) sts. Work 8 rows in pattern without shaping. BO. Rejoin yarn to sts on holder. Maintaining pattern, work 20 sts for front neck and place on st holder. Work in pattern to end of row. Continuing in pattern, dec 1 st at neck edge every other row 3 times—20 (23, 26) sts.

Buttonhole Band

Change to smaller needles and work 4 rows K2 P2 ribbing.

Buttonhole row: * K2, P2, K2, yo, P2tog, repeat from * 1 (1, 2) times, rib to end of row. Work 3 more rows K2 P2 ribbing. BO.

Sleeves

With smaller needle, CO 26 (30, 32) sts. Work Border Pattern in Rows. Change to larger needles and work in Garter Rib Pattern, increasing 1 st at beginning and end of every 4th row 10 times—46 (50, 52) sts. Continue without shaping until sleeve measures 6" (6½", 7½"). BO.

Neckband

Sew front to back at left shoulder. With smaller needle, pick up 8 sts along back shoulder button band, knit 26 sts from holder at back neck, pick up 13 sts down left front neck, knit 20 sts from holder at front neck, and pick up 13 sts long right front neck and buttonhole band—80 sts. Work 1 row K2, P2 ribbing. Make buttonhole in second row as follows: Rib to last 4 sts, yo, P2tog, K2. Work 2 more rows of K2 P2 ribbing. Work 5 rows st st. BO loosely.

Finishing

Sew left sleeve to armhole edge, matching center of sleeve to shoulder seam. Lap buttonhole band over button band and sew together at side edge. Sew right sleeve to armhole edge, matching center of sleeve to top edge of buttonhole band. Sew side and sleeve seams. Sew buttons opposite buttonholes.

TIP
You may want to wind off some yarn so the right front neck starts at the same point in the color sequence as the left front neck, balancing your colors on either side.

Hat

Hat

With smaller needles, CO 88 (104) sts. Join into a circle, being careful not to twist the sts. Work Border Pattern In Rounds.

Change to larger needles and work in Garter Rib Pattern until piece measures 4" (4½"), ending with row 1 of Garter Rib Pattern.

Shape Crown

Round 1: * K2, P2tog, repeat from * to end of round.
Round 2, 4 and 6: K.
Round 3: * K2tog, P1, repeat from * to end of round.
Round 5 and 7: * K2tog, repeat from * to end of round.

Break yarn, draw it through the remaining 11 (13) sts, pull tight to close top of hat, and fasten off on inside.

Booties

Cuff

CO 36 (40) sts. Divide evenly on 3 needles and join, being careful not to twist. Work Border Pattern In Rounds. Work 2 more rows of K2, P2 rib.

Divide for Heel

K 18 (20) sts. Turn work and purl these 18 (20) sts, leaving remaining 18 (20) sts on hold for instep. Work in st st for 1¾", ending with a RS row.

Turn Heel

Row 1 (WS): Sl 1, P10 (11), P2tog, P1, turn.
Row 2: Sl 1, K5, K2tog, K1, turn.
Row 3: Sl 1, P6, P2tog, P1, turn.
Row 4: Sl 1, K7, K2tog, K1, turn.
Row 5: Sl 1, P8, P2tog, P1, turn.
Row 6: Sl 1, K9, K2tog, K1—12 sts remain on heel.
Row 7 (Larger Size Only): Sl 1, P10, P2tog, turn.
Row 8 (Larger Size Only): Sl 1, K10, K2tog.

> **TIP**
> *If you want the color placement on your booties to match, be sure to start both at the same place in the color sequence.*

Gussets

Pick up 9 sts down left side of heel flap. Knit 18 (20) sts for instep. Pick up 9 sts up right side of heel flap. Knit 6 sts from heel. Redistribute your sts so needle 1 starts in the center of the heel and holds 15 sts, needle 2 holds the 18 (20) instep sts, and needle 3 holds 15 sts and ends at the center of the heel—48 (50) sts total.

Gusset Round 1

Needle 1—K.
Needle 2—K0 (2), [P2, K2] 4 times, P2.
Needle 3—K.

Gusset Round 2

Needle 1—K to last 3 sts, K2tog, K1.
Needle 2—K.

Needle 3—K1, SSK, K to end of round.

Alternate Gusset Rounds 1 and 2 until 36 (40) sts remain. Continue without shaping, working in st st on needles 1 and 3, and Garter Rib Pattern on needle 2, for 1" (1¾"), ending with a plain knit row.

Shape Toe

Changing to st st on needle 2, shape toe as follows:

Toe Round 1

Needle 1—K to last 3 sts, K2tog, K1.
Needle 2—K1, SSK, K to last 3 sts, K2tog, K1.
Needle 3—K2, SSK, K to end of round.

Toe Round 2

K all sts.

Alternate Toe Round 1 and 2 until 16 (20) sts remain. K sts on needle 1—your yarn is now at the side of the foot. Slip sts from needle 3 onto needle 1—you now have 8 (10) sts on needle 1 and 8 (10) sts on needle 2. Graft toe closed with kitchener stitch, or turn to inside and close the toe with 3-needle bind off.

Lana Grossa Meilenweit Sock Yarn
Style and Color Used—By Project

Project	Shown on Page	Yarn Style/Color
Baby Gift Set	66-69	Fun and Stripes/630
Baby Gift Set	65, 70-71	Fun and Stripes/632
Bull's Eye Heel Socks	40	Jacquard/408
Dog Sweater	29, 30	Fantasy/4760
Drawstring Bag	53, 54	Multiringel/5040
Fingerless Gloves (Ribbed Cuff)	25	Safari/2020
Fingerless Gloves (Ruffled Cuff)	22	Cotton Multiringel/2210
Fingerless Gloves (Ruffled Cuff)	72	Fantasy/4820
Gauntlets	17, 20	Fun and Stripes/626
Gloves	18, 75	Fantasy/4830
Her Modular Scarf	9, 11	Fantasy/4730
His Striped Scarf	9, 14	Fun and Stripes/621
Leg Warmers	4	Fantasy/4760
Leg Warmers	38, 39	Multiringel/5090
Lightweight Socks	34	Cotton Fun and Stripes/337
Mittens	27, 75	Multiringel/5030
Poncho	57, 63	Fantasy/4710
Sideways Hat	45, 49	Multieffekt/3010
Skater Beanie	46	6 Fach Fun and Stripes/901
Stocking Cap	50	Multieffekt/3070
Thicker Socks	33, 36	6 Fach Multi Jacquard/703
Thicker Bull's Eye Heel Socks	42	6 Fach Multi Jacquard/702
Vest	58, 61	Multieffekt/3010

Lana Grossa Meilenweit sock yarns are available at fine knitting stores.

For a store near you, call Unicorn Books and Crafts at 1-800-289-9276.

Abbreviations

beg—beginning

BO—bind off

CO—cast on

dec—decrease

dbl dec (double decrease)—sl 2 sts together as if to knit them together, k1, pass 2 slipped sts over the last stitch.

K—knit

K2 P2 ribbing—Every Round: * K2, P2, repeat from * to end of round.

K2tog—knit 2 stitches together

K3tog—knit 3 stitches together

m1 (make 1)—use the tip of your left needle to lift up the strand running between the stitch just worked and the next stitch; knit into the back of this strand, twisting the loop to avoid making a hole.

pm—place marker

P—purl

P2tog—purl 2 stitches together

psso—pass the slipped stitch over the st just knitted

RS—right side

sl—slip

SSK (slip, slip, knit)—slip 1 st as if to knit; slip another st as if to knit; slip both sts back to left hand needle and knit them together through back loop.

st st (stockinette stitch)—when working in rows, knit the right side rows and purl the wrong side rows; when working in the round, knit every round.

sts—stitches

WS—wrong side

yo (inc)—yarn over needle

About the Author

Sandi Rosner learned to knit when she was 18 from the instructions in the back of a magazine. She made the leap from hobby knitter to professional in 2000 when she opened Knitting Workshop, a yarn store in Sebastopol, California. Sandi has designed for Crystal Palace and Alchemy Yarns. Her designs can be seen in Knit 'n Style Magazine, Jamieson's Shetland Knitting Book 3, Simply Shetland and Simply Knit 2. This is her first book. Sandi lives in Sebastopol with her teenaged son, Joe.